BLACK ICE

BLACK ICE

Kerry Shawn Keys

BLACK SPRUCE PRESS

Black Spruce Press

Copyright © 2020 by Kerry Shawn Keys. All rights reserved.
Author photograph © 2018 Kyva Adelė Keys. All rights reserved.

ISBN 978-1-7338882-3-3

Manufactured in the United States of America

Black Spruce Press
blacksprucepress.org
blacksprucepress@gmail.com
Design by forgetgutenberg.com

Cover painting by Gonçalo Ivo, *O Lago Negro*, watercolor and collage on paper,
29 x 15 cm, 2000.

Acknowledgements:

Tao te ching Meditations, Bones & Buzzards, book
Poetry International, San Diego, anthology
Conversations With Tertium Quid, book
Druskininkai Poetic Fall, anthology
Devouring The Green, anthology
Poem Hunter, on-line
Spork Press
Red Pagoda Broadsides

CONTENTS

To the duende of the Friday evening Flamenco Kitchen in the Burg going on 3 decades uninterrupted in Ziza and Rick's home... where the Black Ice melts.

You

You look around You.
We are the same.

Your friend on the diving board
at the motel pool.
Your wife submerged in chlorine
in the pool.
Kids playing possum
and hide-and-seek
trying to fool.

The dead are the same.
Look around you.

Your friend on the gangplank
above the pool.
Your wife's hair floating
like seaweed in the pool.
Kids playing dead
and hide-and-seek
trying to fool.

The dead are the same.
Different details come to light.
You gaze, then mirror your gaze
in the mirror.

THE VEHICLE

It's so dark. A moonless, starless night.
And the electricity out, out. Not a candle
in the house, no pack of matches, luster,
no flashlight, no Christmas Eve mouse. Yes,
no dad carrying you piggy-back up these steps
to the room where you once dreamt and slept,
that island of almost Wordsworthian innocence.
You already know all, all of this, this nothingness
of a presence that pockmarks a past now all amiss,
as you hypnotically go down the creaking staircase,
fingers tracing the splotched and violating braille
of the bullet-pitted-marked flowery papered wall,
following the grain of the bannister so as not to fall
or get lost, and then the soft landing on the carpet,
and you know which way to turn to cross
the living room, to cry, and there's no God to help,
no Muse or Virgil or Mother Goose or burning bush,
and you find the oval doorknob and turn it and step out
into another darkness that sucks and swallows you
and your past life and future until a pair of headlights
of an approaching vehicle veer and find you out,
but you don't see them, having already gone blind
staring into the broken horror of sunlight that loomed
inside the sheltered, galactic womb of your bedroom.

Black Ice

Turn off the lights, all of them,
until it's pitch dark as a marble tomb,
and then open the gate toward the mirror.
You know how to get there,
as if drawn by the lodestone
of the North Star's pearly ring.
Fingers' intuition will lead you on,
following table-top to bureau
past blind faith, and fate,
and then to another gate
until you reach out at the end
and touch the cool surface of the face,
the black ice you are certain must be there.
Timeless, cosmetic, perfection's façade.
Then say the required mantra:
Sir, give me a face like yours,
pure darkness, to carry back into the light,
a dimensionless, sinless birthmark, birthright.

TOM THE DOUBTER

Tom The Doubter

And the angel asked me then,
Tom, do you want to begin?
and I put my finger in
out through the hole
to feel what might be real,
and it was so cold
I turned to him and said,
I'm no longer in doubt,
but for the love of God
I won't go, no.

Tom The Doubter, A Sequel

We heard you, Tom.
We know you all too well.
Bardo-land doesn't want you anymore.
Watching your finger stick out the hole,
we grabbed it,
and pulled you through.

ASLEEP

"against the dark, a tall white fountain played"

A knife slices through the windowpane
giving zest to incoherent dreams,
and shards of yellow stars glisten
like barbed-wire across a brick wall,
like so many tiny tongues of succubi
mistaking sleep's supine position
as that of someone waiting to be born
again or to have a battery of children.
Suddenly, you think you are awake,
and look! there drifting in the offing
a battered sail on a skeleton's rigging.
Too late, you think, I've missed the boat.
Or is it the rigging of just one more special effect?
The tip of the knife vanishes into your throat,
a steel-blue droplet trickling into a moat,
but nothing seems real enough to hurt.
Gingerly, one foot and then the other foot
depart your body and the bed, testing the floor,
then tiptoe without you toward the door
heading toward some dicey outer sanctum.
You sense that Paradise might be their destination
as the room begins to rock and reel and suddenly
they are a pair of snake eyes on a crooked ceiling
drenched in human blood, and on reaching up
to squash them, plastic man, arms getting longer
and longer like your children's gluey boric slime,
your fingers get cut to the bone, and this time
you swear you are awake, though disarranged.
Daylight, budding spoiler, aims a laser beam in
just as some ex machina pulls the curtain across
the broken pane, making your dream impregnable,
an ovulating stillborn, internal, composting androgyne.

Coda: and then again I awoke to paper and pen.

LONGING

Impossible in words
to tell what it's like.
One phoneme would be better.
One flea bursting with blood.
Red wine keeps the heart in tune.
The moon seems to be a gigantic spore,
contagious, poised to strike outside the window.
I am shooting a game of pool against myself.
I don't know who I am rooting for.
Framed, shifty table. Smoky haze.
Rules amazingly simple. I look
into my eyes and watch
the cue ball spin

and careen over the green felt of the world.

THE CREATURE

To protect my image, how's that possible
now, floating in the measured saltwater
of this outdoor, special admission aquarium,

my tutelary Gods wagering bets above
as though their pet raven and dove were each
a haruspex, and my body Noah's boat.

I can't escape this worldly exhibition.
There's no gate, and anyway the hectic light
of jacklights would poach me vessel and soul

wherever I might even hope to go.
Once I had a compass, a tailwind, a cross breeze
but now my home is empty-handed except for me.

Only when the sun goes down and the audience
returns to its own element, sated and benign in its
dream of me, do I have a chance for mine.

Then I lie on my back, bloated buoyant with desire,
my own island, my own Robinson Crusoe,
discovering in the stars the larvae of Lascaux.

Consolation Prize

for K.P.

I listen to the birds fly by of course.
I'm indifferent to the ways of women and men.
I tell them of course what there isn't to know,
      and my blood freezes over from drinking
      the slow water of their dreams.
She was taking a sponge-bath in her father's brain.
If you were to live like me, the sun would drop runic arrows
      in your throat. You'd sprout plumes and zippers.
I gave her a blue ribbon for her squirming epiphanies.
What do you know of pleasure or pain.
We are eating an apple in a stable at the racetrack
      but your hands and head will be severed.
Your mouth is painted with Elmer's Glue.
A cow migrates from the Indus to Europe.
You will piss from a hole decorated with black flags.
Your tongue is a dead snake in unsloughed pantaloons.
I eat the birds flying over the classifications and the buzzings,
      the trains and the hyperventilating volcanoes.
They give me money for my services.
Is the sky blue. I will take this pumice and crush it
      with my teeth into little people. Watch.
Cicero is a raindrop. Babel a papermill.
I am a pebble in a fountain on a mountain. Children love
      rhythm and rhyme, come to me in and out of time.
The body when it separates from the soul perishes
      in a Heaven of sheep.
The soul stays behind, chirping, chirping, chirping,
      like a bird at a street-crossing for the blind.

KINETOSIS

cedars sliced by the vehicle's windshield
the air conditioner drips invisibly on the macadam and the mud
the colors green and white and amber, or blue and silver, enter
       the eyes' lanterns mixing with fire and water
the flag pole waves a resinous negligee
       washing the empyrean, and the window sprouts
       its own cracked blossoms
the inside of life is the speed of language,
       the outside of language smashes the frontal lobe
       with the church bell ripped from the rear-view mirror
how all the passengers want to join the couple there on the hillside
       and come between them over and over
       as they gather up their commune which, though light
       and airy, adds a minimalist depth to the bigger picture
later the voyeurs all enlisted and thrust their pigstickers into
       the infidel's trunk and groin
a loose thread of the conversation attaches itself to a needle
       and swims upstream into the womb of the monastery
the flowchart on the dashboard measures the distance
between each obituary tree and alternates
with the digital photography and the bridge work
First-aid is given to the body bags as the firemen bend over
       the empire's eclipse, their heads involved in the havoc
       of the emanations
the funeral is magnificent and magnanimous
the specialists open up the trunk of the tree of life and penetrate
       the tinted, jade eyeglasses of the higher-elevation tourists
       that are poised to slide down and pass through the hole
       in the dike to their immense destruction and recreation

AFFINITY WITH BEANS

Geometry is easier to master, plain or solid,
than this outline of ligaments and bones,
this lush landfill of flesh and blood, sex and death.
Still, nothing dies in realms we can't imagine.
Last evening, I cooked potatoes and kale
and a fish fresh from the creek.
All quickly went to mush in my stomach.
Did they find another life there, a congenial rebirth,
or were they merely eaten away
by the acids of nothingness into a nauseous mortality.
Is the potato soul, the kale soul, the fish soul
out in the garden or in the creek, or pleading
in the kitchen or in the outhouse in a reek of compost.
Or do souls exist individually everywhere at once
exempt from pain and every nuance of change.
Part of my supper by now has become part of my flesh,
and should a soul be inseparable from its tenure,
do all these souls share my sense of oblivion,
of our time asleep being our only redemption.
Sometimes, overcome by drink, I blurt out my longing
to touch this quirky quiddity that can't be touched—
the ultimate taboo, an infinite tautology, or I conjure
the soul as round and blue, and something to dissolve in
as if into a deep pool of moonlight. And then
posthaste I see the awful fantasy, the romantic escapism
of an imagination and life wedded to the routine
of reverie and the incestuous nest of the self.
Better to fixate on the absurdity of it all and redress the issue.
Really, Pythagoras was right—the soul does have a mundane
affinity with beans, but I suspect it rejoices in them
as a mechanism for escaping us, though we might wish
to the contrary, imagining ourselves the dream of a butterfly
hovering within our every inspiration.
Tonight, after a meal of beans fresh from the garden,
I can smell my soul's gone AWOL for the while,
and I don't mind at all—it's over there struggling
in the bamboo, ah there it is in the butterfly weed,
and now it's flying around the redbud and the rose of Sharon,
oh here it is coughing blood in my hands like an unhealthy
prodigal son maybe wanting to return. My womb's
not so generous, and my hands are too busy on their own track
trying to separate themselves from accident and corruption,
and my mind's enjoying the visuals of the game.

Really, who needs the elusiveness of a soul when Death gives us
the only definition we need within the outline of our body
chalked in advance on the asphalt of our daily commute.
The soul after all is a lazy vagrant at heart, and will, unmindful,
find its way back into the soup kitchen of our brainpan,
and again feast on the empty rice bowl of its ruminations.

SCRIPTORIUM

It's cold in here.
Silent. I can't hear anything
other than the blue thrum
of distant blood coursing
against the pen.

It's cold in here.
Cold comfort dear Death at least
would be warmer,
drone of decomposition creating
a nest of energy and fire.

It's cold in here.
Black box heart and graybearded brain
at loss for a conversation.
They're at loose ends, mourning
the soul that once bonded them.

STANDING OUTSIDE THE DREAM

Standing outside the dream
and looking in,
I see the dead on all sides.
looking down
through me until their eyes collide
with twigs and snow and the prismatic spill
of a bottle of snake oil
where someone stashed my portfolio.
In their hands, my documents.
It's clear I'm also part of their dream,
and they're looking up through me—not down—
into the blue, monotonous sky.
It is our secret hungering, the scalpel of appetite
for immortality
that brings us so charmed
as if hypnotized
into the vicious circling of our being.
We embrace by embracing
the space between us
hoping to outwit the notion
that the dead die too.
Eyes search in slow motion
the remnants of time.
We hear the wind whine
like Hell's hounds on the run
before all goes still and fog
drapes the dream,
and the dream's dream
along with
the seas and the mountains,
the fountains and the trees,
the pantomime of God's house of glass and sand.
Holding a crumpled map in one hand,
thumbing the air with the other,
I join their spectacle
and look around to where I had been,
glimpsing for one last moment
our gestures, our genius, our expectancy
on the radar screen.

RESPONSE TO C. MIŁOSZ

in reference to the "Second Space"

How vast this universe, this earth.
Walk around, soar into the sun,
crumple a beer can on the moon.
Trees, flowers, bees, birds, Homo Sapiens
and other weeds, some of these are left.

The soul blossoms in a heartbeat,
and then disappears in a stroke.
Up is a skyscraper scratching the Great Bear.
Down, death bubbling and turning sour
like yeast in a root cellar.

Have we really lost faith in the world.
O' yes, it vanished millenniums ago
into a preference for Heaven and Hell.

How to find salvation in Guantanamo Bay or a living cell.
And the damned, don't they live like most, parasites
in one another's assholes in the watercloshes of Black Sites.

Why should we weep. Nothing's been lost.
Why rejoice. Nothing's been found.

Look around you. Love your dog more than yourself.
When flesh sinks into compost, what's left but nothing else.

INTERACTIVE DIORAMA

Here on this concrete island
no bigger than my feet,
when I fall to sleep
(please push the button)
I fall down.
Icy water splashes
clean through to the bone.
A few times more,
then bullets pour through the skull.
(please push the button
for the cold ground
to carry me home)
(please push the button
to exit the exhibit)
(please push the button
if it's raining)
(please push the button
for an umbrella)
(please push the button
for a limo home)

ORDERS

for J.L.B.

from an uncertain, classified manual

Organisms Are Divided Into:

1 belonging to the General
2 amputated
3 between airplanes and the ocean
4 tamed
5 toad-suckers
6 what from very close cannot be seen
7 beached
8 didactic
9 red wharf-rats with fleas
10 not included in future classifications
11 cowardly
12 one-winged birds tangled in webs
13 extinct
14 painted with a very sharp knife
15 et alibi
16 having just broken its bones
17 what from very far away looks like a mutilated egg.

Ringing the Dead

We were speaking to the dead,
some of us didn't know it, of course.
Some of us did.
Some were in suspended animation,
others, in a suspension of disbelief,
believed now in everlasting Hell
on earth and damnation.
I was calling Rose.
Others, their Alegria, their Felice,
their Constance, their Alexander, their Angel,
etcetera, etcetera, in the same vein.

The explosion took them by surprise.
Their throats exploded into fiery snakes,
arms and legs baked on the spot.
Heads banged against charcoaled faces,
genitals against rocks.
Fingers crawled away in the dust.
Tongues screamed in tongues.
Bridesmaids married death.

Rose Rose Rose Rose her cell phone called.
Alegria Alegria Alegria are you there.
Felice Felice Felice my darling answer,
who's with you my darling. I'll kill you both.
Angel, your mother, get yourself home, Now.
Alex I love you.
Rose Rose Rose.

None will rise.

When they took the ropes down
that cordoned off the site,
I went over with a broom.
I swept up a dustpan of spores,
nameless now, and sifted them
into a tiny, golden box.

Open sesame, Open sesame,
our children pray.
A convert, I pray to Pandora
and curse God for taking Rose away.

Looking Out

the outside North looking in
that expanse of light
filling my eyes and the room
an ideal light I'm told
for making images of the world

that may be
there's nothing painterly about me

instead I stand here in this script
looking out
at the Athens of the North
the chimney tops and bricks the smoke

the bone-ash pastel of dusk's nondescript brushstroke

the faucet drips
                    haphazardly

stray tomcat spray
marks the entranceway
so that nowadays the angel of death stays away
as do the seraphim and Purim puppet plays

evening's getting dark now
and my hungry eye barely makes out
the drab zodiacs of antennae

the moon sets to the side of the frame
felt but unseen

planets are playing charades as satellite disks

barely audible
dirges and dybbuks hum in the shoal of the urban buzz

of time and space and emptiness

and I listen as best I can
locked inside myself
unknowable smoldering motionless
looking out

THE CURSE

Black mold on the wall in the kitchen, presque vu,
in the former Jewish ghetto in tonight's upper room
drunken delirium, the blood of Rabbi Christ
surfacing as frescoed pentimento long hidden.

Two forks on the table, a bread knife, a bottle
of Manischewitz skimmed from holy water,
commune a still-life out of death, palms and thigh
pierced, immured on the other side of the other side.

Smog and heavy clouds turn the overcast sky
into sickly shades of a dusty monsoon yellow.
One tree across the way, not named yet by Adam
or me, spreads out its bloody braille of bare branches.

The silence is so stale, it breaks into small pieces.
The withered mums in the vase choke for water.
If there is such a thing as a splendid guardian angel,
it is no more than exiled fallen light, tonight.

ANT HILLS

Ant hills at the pits of Ponar.
And here on Lowland Street
an ant departs from under
the floorboards, its sticky feet
heading towards the forest.
Antennae know the way by heart
on the darkest of nights from the garret.
I sleepwalk after them by flashlight.
Other nights, moonlight and the satellite
in my tablet are enough equipment
to feed the morbid zakhor of our detachment.

They Measure Time

they measure time in their way
they measure blood
they measure death
inside a stork's wings
inside the heartbeat of flies

they measure ozone over Russia
the monarchs on their way to Mexico
the mutilation in the black sites
the cubic feet of Guantánamo Bay
the Cossacks and Tartars in the Crimea

they measure death

they measure how many meters to the end of the world
they measure how slippery it is there
and how far one can drop on a cloudy day
they measure the body heat of the tortured
the blood pressure of placenta and rats and children
how long it takes to confess innocence
how long it takes to be innocent
how long it takes to confess guilt
how long it takes to squeal
how long it takes to kill
how long it takes to be an angel or a pig

they measure death

bleeding to death
falling to death
suffocating to death
being pummeled to death
pleading for death

and then
and then they decide
and then they decide to measure the measure

and so they set out for the Dogon
but a drone gets there before them
the dogs are all dead
the villagers are all dead
the villages are nowhere to be seen
the stars have been herded into a pen and burned.

THE SEER

We know or at least we want to know
that Homer, likely, did not write down
his tales, that he was blind, or at least
blind toward the end of his song.
Or was it Demodokos that did the singing.
I think it doesn't matter, and so this meandering
in order to give myself the privilege
of interrupting myself and asking a few things
above all others that have captivated my imagination:
what was the last composition that he saw,
that is, if he ever had the gift of seeing,
and what was the last word he might have written
if he had ever written a word, and above all, for this
we surely cry out to know, what was the last sound
he made before he died. Was it a kind of music,
a lullaby of weeping charmed into a single phoneme,
or was it more like the sustained gurgle of a death-rattle
rising from a Hector or an Achilles battling
for air in the bottomless dregs of his lungs.

DEATH SHOULD BE INTIMATE

Death should be intimate.
It should be something like this—
sitting in a rocking chair,
mistaking the wings of an angel
for the swish of the rocker.

It should be sitting down for dinner,
the white napkins, the soup of bread and garlic,
a soup spoon approaching the mouth,
and then suddenly falling forward,
the wine glass spilling on your lap
at the moment of death, and the glass
breaking on the floor the moment after.

It should be in bed, again the color white,
this time the white sheets and the pillow case,
dawn bringing its alba song of love through the window,
with the sun barely visible behind pink clouds,
and then you see your body beneath,
curled up in sleep like a fetus on the bed,
and you are floating above, slowly, slowly
in the thermal, in shafts of sunlight.

And finally, after dying so many times,
death might be a knife, hidden, intangible
in such a shaft of sunlight, silver, invisible,
a secret knife, not yours, not the kitchen's,
not the beloved's, but belonging to someone like Abraham,
a servant of a god, a myth, or belonging to no one,
self-contained in its intimacy, eternal, waiting for nothing,
and, yes, your soul, which is all that is left of you,
will pass through it on its way.

KIEFER'S

fertility of brick and lead
not grass or worm

fertility of weeds
dry dry as sunlight
drawn and quartered
into the skin of stone

fertility of human beings
bones fertilizing bones

DUST TO DUST

You can use a steel brush,
you can take bleach and ammonia,
baking soda and vinegar, sandpaper,
Mary Magdalene's hair, spit, a lemon,
boiling water or lye, Heaven,
a razor, scissors, paint, paint thinner,
revisionist gobbledygook, whitewash of fire,
or take them all together—
you'll never trick that monster, Death,
from dragging you and everything you love
like some hapless Hector
through a brutal and inconceivable dust.

BLACK BAG

in memory of my Aunt Margie

Often I too casually daydreamed I would drape
and pull airtight over my head and neck
a plastic trashbag blacker than the mind's
midnight mined malignant anthracite,

Until one night, hunched over, pissed, face to face
with a black bag jerry-rigged Christo-like
on the cracked porcelain of a public toilet,
I repulsed the mirror of myself in that palette.

SHIPWRECK

now to hear "the breath of the night wind..."
—Matthew Arnold

for Johannes Bobrowski

Cataracts of clouds like snow.
Night dilates, shimmers on the wall of trees
through the crystal breath of the moon.
Sand and sea shift into one.
A fish leaves its imprint in a pebble. A bird
swims through its grey shadow in the spruce.
Something moves and dives
into its own movement.
The sun is a tiny gleam
hidden in a dark ring on the other side
of the world.
The dead drift in low across wracked grass,
part mist, part dew.
It's cold, so cold, that we
rig together the bones
from the graveyard of dunes.
We will build a fire to lure their ghosts
back home.

HEAT LIGHTNING

it comes and goes all evening long
flashes like nails sprung from a coffin
riddles the eyes clear to the socket-bone

it's a party Halloween the end of the world
you turn to Saint Sebastian and ask for the last dance
instead he pulls an arrow from his heart

and sails it toward a little pukka
immersed in the spangled clouds
it ricochets into Christ's heart

and you transubstantiate
into a wafer and wine
and offer yourself to the crossroads

one last time...

HOFFERS

I know very little of the Hoffers, Helvetian half-mast ancestors.
I know they were mountain goats and masons and not farmers.
Their mission was mortar and stone, not dung and fodder.
They spoke a language heavy like stone, a marbled tongue,
granite and limestone mixing guttural Bach with Palatinate,
Deitsch, Appalachia, jugband English and Scots.
I don't know much more about them other than
that they were like my father, all of them orphans.
Their fathers and grandfathers, also doubtless, itinerant orphans,
persecuted in their homeland to be rebaptized Pennsylvanian.
Who knows, indeed, what happened to any of them, simply gone,
as all of us sometime, inhabitants of a dollopy land called Oblivion.
Though now and then they occupy my mind, craggy phantoms
building dry stone walls through the quicksand of my poems.

South Mountain

"what must I sing"

I will settle in South Mountain.
Passers-by call it the Blue Mountain
though it's orange as a phoenix in Autumn,
and in Winter grey and barren.

There all the apples are windfallen
and the women electric and cloven.
I will settle in South Mountain
where flocks of shorn stars are gathering.

The sun skirts the trees in a fountain
of light, the moon in creation's green.
I will settle in South Mountain
where whippoorwill and nightingale mingle to sing.

I will settle in South Mountain.
No angel fallen or risen
could ever begin to imagine
better bearings to awaken Eden.

I will settle in South Mountain.
No gate there or grace or praying
to separate Hell from Heaven.
The unborn and dead call it the Blue Mountain.

WHAT DOES THE MOUNTAIN CARE

Her halo inhales too many harpies into its orbit.
She turns her face but where is her heartbeat.
The service gets old, the fig-leaves, falcons, and loaves of bread
are already routine, the letters Y and K tumble,
followed by all their disciples, from the dictionary.
In time, the external freak is a snail unwinding
a ball of yarn caught in a cat's claw next to Neptune's Fountain.
It's so slimy, and the dinner utensils rebel and crisscross
more and more often, and death propagates like my moustache
smeared with stolen milk and oily dust from a ceiling of nudes.
The ferry service has also stopped. The sea is frozen over,
and now fish are busy swallowing fish, and the world
is overpopulated with seagulls and dead people and empty nets.
I put spoonfuls of mistletoe and worms on the line,
trying to catch George Sand's grandfather, but the room
is too dark, clouded with red chalk; and candles
are eating away every last cent of oxygen.
At heart, we all should have been Mannerists,
thrown our multiple personalities into unlucky lapdogs,
and painted pupils with pineapples and monkeys,
serenely elegant skulls pigmented with perfume, nocturnes,
and allegories of nudes bending over to fetish our feet.
Of course. But too much of the body's light mixes
with the soul's feathers and blood, and Peterson's Guide
says that this bird's neck resembles a black tie,
and that that bird's legs look like strident strands of redtape.
It says that in a certain season, certain birds from certain flyways
frequent certain bodies of water, and that with devotion
and properly adjusted binoculars, an enthusiast
can occasionally catch a glimpse of a mysterious dove.
I saw one once while out on a count—the sky momentarily cleansed
to an anti-freeze blue by a snowstorm—I saw it
in the stratosphere of forests that on the other side almost reaches
down to spawn in the darkling, close-webbed mist of the sea.

SHE LOOKS IN THE MIRROR

It began with me in my late teens
when my soul seemed to hover in my bosom
like a glistening apple still on the stem.
I was an eternal virgin then in a beautiful kingdom.
Standing before the mirror in the bedroom,
I would stare at the reflection of my face,
dilating my pupils as Houdini had taught me,
letting my eyes relax, though the gaze remained focused
staring back at me with a blank intensity.
No blinking permitted, and the head absolutely stilled.
The door to the room locked so that no persona non grata
would enter to interfere with the masquerade before me.
Slowly, my face took on the image of some sort of
incomprehensible Neanderthal ghoul, and then transfigured
into a kind of fishy snake, something like a pike, and then a lizard,
or both so intermingled that it was hard to tell
which was which or who was who or what was me.
No ambrosia or soma, and I had never taken LSD.
Then finally, the reward that I foresaw was coming
from having practiced this exercise so many times before:
my whole head would disappear though I knew my eyes
were open since I could still see that the mirror was there
reflecting the furnished background of myself before me—
an open window, a rose, a garden gate, and a strange tree.

Ever since, I have on occasion asked others
if they had ever done this vanishing exercise
or decapitation in the field of vision, or would.
A few then tried, but experienced only themselves
in their eternally incredulous good fortune
and not the fish or lizardy ghoul or gorgon,
and never the nothing that had replaced my head.

Perhaps one of the heads that I lost so many times
in the mirror's deep abyss will return to me
as I look into this mirror here before me,
and I will see myself as I once, unrecognized, was:
youthful, handsome perhaps, as a woman almost beautiful
is often said to be, unbruised, a veritable prize for death.
Not this weathered aegis whose dreadful face wizened
by time and stress and the elements, stricken by love and fate,
more and more resembles a non-descript fetus
dreaming in the womb of a young woman dreaming
she is still a virgin, standing headless before an admiring mirror.

Now That I'm A Bird

for Katie F. and Jonas E.

Now that I'm a bird, it's confusing
but wonderful.
The way the sky opens in and out,
thimbleful by thimbleful.
It's grey when it opens in,
green when it opens out.
The wall of trees in the forest
                                    swings
both ways. The sun's door
                                    swings
into my eyes and burns them blue.
Over here is where I go for a hop or to bathe,
and over there is where I stumble
when my love opens the windows.
Other birds with yellow wings are in cages,
my wings are brown
and bigger than raindrops.
Up in the clouds I can see a hawk
sharpening its twelve knives. I drag my foot
around in a shoe in a circle to distract
the dangers of the world.
Someone is drooling on the leafy blinds
and spreading birdlime on the knobs of the trees.
Is there a door for you, wings? I think out loud,
repeating that refrain to myself.
When I tire of such gobbledygook, I fly in through
the cellar window and hide under a discarded cradle
with a hoard of Mason jars and binoculars.
Often there's a little boy there, curled up
like a fetus or broken umbrella. We munch on a nightcrawler
together and then take off through the darkness
like the headlights of a car.
Then the down on my breast is softer than moonlight,
my breath marvelous with myrrh.
And the sky is greener than a bed of lettuce,
and the boy transposed into a gleaming God.
I call him Adonis. I call him Winter and Summer.
We sail around the terrestrial globe
dropping leaflets inside balloons.
Someone sticks one with a pin.
The message says, There was a civil disturbance.

BIRDS

There are birds everywhere, feasting on my days,
on every windy sill and angle, solid as steel
in their still geometry, or unreal as gossamer
and Spanish moss when they flit lazily about the trees,
twig to twig, in a watery haze of sun and leaves.
Nothing's more certain than they've come back
for me, the dim din and dazzle of their wings
reflecting from the starry apron of heaven
into our identical, elliptical, tidal migration.
Flow. Flow on, the body invents a temporary home
until flowing, flowing on, it succumbs, leaves
the center of the frame like a leaf or these birds falling
branch to branch, plumes of snow, lizards of rain.
The spirit may be holy but it's weak. Pretty boy,
pretty boy, it releases its claws from wooden spindle
and flies distilled and antiseptic toward the interminable.
Far away in time I see Lazarus ascending from the grime
of earth into the fire-baked clay of man again.
He's climbing, rung by rung, listless, braindead, wingless,
not wanting to come back into flesh as he must
in order to touch for us the Pentecostal gaze of heaven.
Inversed, these birds descend, cloud by cloud, from azure
of sky into the webby green panoply of earth's eye.
And I'm standing by, grounded but wired like a puppet
in between their disparate, contiguous realities,
drawn and quartered between Heaven and Hell
more a neutered angel or wood-carved speechless Pinocchio
in some Brancusi's or Pygmalion's birdcage of a studio
than fiery Prometheus delivered over to vultures
on a mountainside or a Sisyphus struggling up a hill.

QUIET NIGHT

It's a quiet night.
A quiet night
    to sit and listen
to the pain of the world.
      It
makes so much noise.
      But
I am tired of trying
and close my eyes
to the pain of the world,
my ears
to the pain of the world.

It's a quiet night
    to sit and hear
my heart beating
   its eardrum
   from within.
But I am tired of trying,
    and deaf
    and numb.
Let the quiet night listen.

ELSEWHERE

Striding water,
this is what
light does
at the high-tide
of its eminence,
but this evening
when the sky
burns its
burnished pastel
into the earth's soul,
who should stride what.
The sun sets
like some huge
carnivorous insect
going elsewhere to hunt.
I keep my eye on it,
our orbits crisscrossing,
but it ignores mine.
I watch the night
for the starlight
to flick its daggers
into my heart—I like that.
Better yet, to sink
into the moonlit clouds
as if into water,
and who would stride then
not to think to drown
into the low-tide
of such a death,
so serene, so clean
of the world
and its pain.

BLACK CURTAINS

...and the daymare said: I will forthright kill....... and myself
        if any suspicion of this gets out

and she desired:

black curtains over the windowpane

black sheets around the crib to make a coffin

black night covering bedroom door

black paint across ceiling and floor

and he endured:

walled in by darkness and death

as I flow past my children into the world of the deaf

and dumb to join the asylum

of the underworld in Tiresias' eyeless mind

her/his longing

his/her dream

THINGS

There are no names for them,
for those some that are referred to
as the unborn, those others as poor things
that were born to doom at home,
in clinics, in a side street, or the john.
No one has ever set up a stone
since not even God spoke to them.
Perhaps they were lucky, in forfeit
not to live on, but I doubt it—so soon
did earth smack its lips again.

THE CAUL OF DARKNESS

at the end of the reeds
at the bottom of the lake
at the bottom of our world
as we know it

where I read the passing
of fish the passing of time
the passing of pages of thoughts
never expressed or gone to press

here I sit floating in the universe
for whatever is and isn't
here I squat by the lake
gills and scales long gone

shivering cold and empty
brimstoned brimful Jobless rich

PEBBLE

Perhaps it was such a pebble
with which Cain killed Abel.

Perhaps such a pebble
pelted by a youth
slew Goliath.

Perhaps it was such a pebble
that was thrown over a shoulder.

Perhaps such a pebble
is the daughter of a boulder
that over and over
rolls down a hill.

Perhaps such a pebble
played hopscotch and pocket-pool
with Beckett and Cortázar
in a Paris bazaar.

Perhaps such a pebble
is buried in a nook
in the Wailing Wall
or shook
in the confines of Jericho.

Perhaps such a pebble
was born in the sea
of tranquility
and the stillness
of eternity.

Perhaps such a pebble
gave birth to the sea
which then bore you and me.

Perhaps such a pebble
is a pebble after all
and the child
of a rose and a stone
and a pebble is a pebble
is a pebble is the bone
of the earth and a koan.

Morning Panorama Reverie

and the grass that grows long in the evening
    and fondles the icy stars, lies damp
        in the dew in the morning,
            asleep on the earth
and the silver birch across the way
    weeping in morning's coral sunlight,
        weeps at night, sweeping the moon
           with yellowing leaves
and the sun drifting across the tiffany blue sky
    satiated from its feast in the dark night,
        caresses the fins of the minnows
        in the lake
and the hop vine above the fence
    strangling the apple tree enticingly in a noose,
        invites me to the liquor cabinet
        to lift a toast to death
and the bucket asleep sideways on the well-cover
    thirsty for the dark liquids of mother earth,
        for the moment bailing
           only the ambergris of its dreams
and the rusty wheelbarrow that wants to be painted red
    and have the neighbor's rooster
        crow from the lectern
        of its handle bars
and the sorrowful rose of sharon with its first buds pinched off
    and thrown into the manger of compost
        with banana peels and corn husks,
           oaten reeds and mushy crab apples,
and the cup of dark roast on the deck
    sip by sip pulsing
        from my mouth
        to my groin
and last:

the embers in the ashes
    in last night's firepit glimmering
        like the down of a phoenix
           greeting the oasis of morning light

FERAL CATS

for Jinjoo, precious pearl

This morning the feral cat
has come to pay a visit,
washing, licking herself
for nearly an eternity
in the dewy, cool grass,
the purslane and applemint.
I want to join in but don't.
Instead, I'll drift barefoot
through her bath to the lake
and bathe with grass snake
and perch and the wild ducks.
Still, she's got me remembering us
in God's Country many years back
making a tumbleweed of the world
rolling over and over wild mint
and clover and a netherworld
of voles, licking, sniffing ourselves,
purring, drunk as cats on catnip.

FLOWERING

Twilight-blue berm aster
  keep your ragged beauty
    as we walk past

Sunlight-yellow dandelion
  bless the lawn's green grass
    with your stubborn insistence

Climbing, trellised clapboard-rose
  keep close to the open window
    and keep close when it's closed

Dahlias soft and fragile
  keep my father's memory
    who loved you most of all

Pink clover butterfly bower
  your heady fragrance
    drifts round the whole earth

Hopvine winding around
  the wild apple tree
    remind me I'm also a trespasser

Rhododendron petals in the stream
  let me eddy and swirl like you
    heading toward the ocean

Tree of Life: we left your benevolence
  for all of this Beauty
    dying around us

WITCH HAZEL

a study in pathology

The two tiny seeds are not hazel.
My eyes are, but these
are black and shiny pupils resting
inside a woody urn, not unlike a pinebox.
We string them to ward off others' evil eyes.
Deer and rabbits eat the twigs, but ungainly creatures
rub the resin in to ward off pain.
Yet what I conjure most is the concoction
in the medicine cabinet, and the word witch.
When we dug a well, we first employed a wizard
with a forked branch for a divining rod.
The water was deep beyond frost and reflection.
The pressure a river of oracle bubbling.
My mind is addicted to homeopathic cures,
quaint charms, powwows, and hill-country religion.
To words as things, to things as words.
To you as me, to me as you.
To prevent nightmares and possession
the first few weeks we slept together,
I hid a branch under the bed,
kept some flowers in a vase nearby,
and after our union, took a beeline to the bathroom
to rub some in over my heart and sex and lungs.

LOVE POEM

A deer bounding across fern and lupine,
fearful, escaping unveiled into the twilight.
I could write poems for her, naked poems, patter
on leaves, nostrils flared, white tail bobbing,
barbwire fence with patches of fur left behind,
the seven holy points of her totemic mate's horns
racked higher than pity or regret in my living room.
That's not what my life now wants or ever did.
I still hope for an almost 'still-life', given, found, not rigged,
not an hourglassed natura morta or our Pieta on the run
even if the destination were immortality, Heaven or beyond.
I want her here close to me, earthly, fearless, nuzzling the air,
closer than life or death, downwind, ears eased downward,
staring, staring through, deep brown eyes, both of us beloved.

Just Biding Time

The lilacs have already bloomed by the doorway
where the rippled darkness of the garden begins,
and bloomed awhile in the vases back home
where regretfully they last but a day or two
though their allusive fragrance looms in the bedroom's
memory sometimes for weeks or years on end.
Cold comfort's new recruits are jasmine. A bitter spring,
late frost killed the apple blossoms in bud,
and now the apple tree stewards me only
as a canopy of leaves to shelter from a short shower
or to sit under for awhile at dusk and gaze
at the madder lake of the sky, and look across the lawn
for a solitary windfall that this year I know
is already forbidden to find. It's a cold July also.
The ragged tips of the lilacs go well with the season's mood,
as does the stunted corn that I suspect also will never
put forth an ear or house a worm in canary kernels of sugar.
Autumn's near-at-hand for sure. The birds are nearly quiet
and some I imagine have gone packing. It's almost
communion in reverse to go down to the dock
and feed the fish with bread from last year's grain—
given this year's rot and rain, the fish I'll feed next year
I don't think will complain should their bread come
from elsewhere, somewhere far away in the larger union
we've become. Seldom do I hear an owl, but tonight there's one.
It must be perched high in the spruce tree closer to heaven,
its keen eye on the nearly full moon squatting over the lake.
The moon is as big as an apple and beautiful and serene.
The owl will let it alone and wait for other game.
I will close the gates, go to bed and dream a forbidden dream—
that this season without so much as passing, has come to an end.

Circuit Of Animals

Aries
What is golden. The horn
or the inflection of the horn,
the spiral of longing
reaching from Earth to Heaven
and back again.
Springtime, my Love, and liaisoned
in a fleece of passion,
we mate and make merry,
burying the Winter
and exhaling the sun.

Taurus
Cut my throat
and you'll still have Europe.
The Pleiades cluster around me
though I live for Venus.
In the hall of Lascaux
my image was trapped
on a wall, not me.
It may be
the imagination wants
yours truly in its bull-ring.
Beware—I am the blood
of the bull and the matador
bellowing together.

Gemini
Bottle-fed,
I watched my sister
at my mother's breast.
She is a thief.
I am a voyeur.
We come together
in the splendor
of the power of the air
****

Brother, don't despair.
I, too, am looking
after you.

Cancer
Don't fear because I wear

my hardware for all to see.
It's thus they don't see me.
Eyeless, darker than the turn
of the solstice, the moon
is my watery friend.
Open my Gate to the Sun.
Follow me into dissolution.

Leo
Often, you have crawled
under my skin, and waved
my tail as if it were a wand.
Would that I were more lucid
than the Sphinx
or more crafty than the fox.
As it is, I am a box
for bees, a regal hieroglyph,
the wishful, sleeping constellation
of tamed dreams, memory
shaped into a constellation.

Virgo
They say I live in Mercury
but I think his quick silver lives in me.
Once I was Mary. Now I am married
to the underworld of Eternity.
When Springtime lands,
take my hand into the flowering fields
and for one brief moment
foster your love again
in dance and song.

Libra
Day and Night,
but which light is mine, yours,
when the body waxes vestigial
and the sting of life
consigns the flesh to strife
not suited
to the dignified absence
of Being.
And what are these apples on your scales,
with no one to claim them
with the Earth turning on its carousel
unconscious of a past,

oblivious to any teleological forecast,
serene in its unknowing.

Scorpio
And so the hunter
is hunted
as we all are,
in the molt of the sun,
by the cold touch
of the moon.
All of us, hanging
out in limbo every day,
signatures of ourselves,
immune to life and decay.
And then as if out of nowhere,
the scorpion appears,
that subtle, venomous theologian,
declaring us heretics,
and the rays of our daily sun
become our coveted whips.

Sagittarius
Bow and rattle
hanging
in the crib of the heavens.
When the bough breaks
the lullaby learns an alibi
for the thrill the brain
tutors from the eye.
Arrow on fire.
Horse, scorpion, birds!
Where is the lyre
that brought us here,
mutable, hips and thighs
entwined in a grievous net of desire.

Capricorn
Out of the stable of the sea,
from water and victory,
I bring you the horn of plenty.
Your father suckled at my breast.
Once I was a fish, but now I climb
each mountain pass, my horns
glittering in the hourglass
of the sun like mirrors
mirroring a splendid emptiness.

Aquarius
Drink
from the stream of air
pouring through
the universe, through you.
You are the cup
bearing yourself to the Gods.
They too will drink, will drown
in the great flood
of your chaos and birth.
Both you and they
always supervising
each other's death.

Pisces
Swimming together
we come apart.
Parted, we join.
You and I
bound and boundless
in the delirious
secret prisons
of ourselves.

CHARTA PERGAMUM

we couldn't find any suitable bark or paper
to chart or redress or roll up this life on earth
nor any reedy papyrus... a circle of devotion
and the authority of blood so surrounded us...
                     and thus asylumed
we notched our initials and passion with teeth and nail and arrow
with burning mirrors
into each other's skin
inside two hearts
and hemmed in the twain to one
and then worded
and drunk with the perfume and fame of this world
boarded a bark for another
far apart from our self-engorged embargo
         and then everything went up in flames
         as if all of Rome and her baths were burning
including the dusty pollen of our love   its fleeting gun powder cargo
and the names of nameless things
though the earth and sea remained
                     and something somewhere
rumbled   or perhaps it should be said
mumbled   it seems good

50. FROM TAO TE CHING MEDITATIONS, BONES & BUZZARDS

Give up the ghost of identity.
It haunts the forests of hubris.
Give the buzzard this day his daily bread.
Let the head of Orpheus
float down the river into the jaws
of the hippopotamus, the razored saws
of carnivorous, Brazilian piranhas.

There are hormones for sprouting wings
and boneblack for deodorizing
various fragments of the imagination.
And there are poets who use pigment
to camouflage their intentions. But how
does one hide from the self within?

The market has bones the color of the moon
that atrophy when the gravity
of movement is gone. Never stall to sell
a song about birth or death

Or the wasteland of loaded dice in between.
Sing about everything that knows no peace.
Sing about the head of Orpheus still thirsting
for Eurydice, bobbing down the Hebrus to the Aegean Sea.

SHE IS ALWAYS THERE

She is always there. I see her
with her brown, twilled sweater
quietly playing a game of hearts
with her life in the opposing chair,

or sometimes sitting on the floor alone
as if she were a discarded card
in a game of solitaire long since lost.

And then looking in the bar's gilded mirror
I see her again, sitting beyond me in a halo
of George Sand smoke rings in Vilnius,

and there is someone in a grey sweater
at the oak table across the way, a peculiar animus,
writing pieces of a poem for her in Sapphics.

The Golden Aquarium

When liminal, where are we going
my Love, are we coming or going.
A little farther on or back to where
we came from, asleep in the womb
or heading into the unknown.
Now, I'm falling asleep here
in a seat high in a musical air
built for two but sitting alone.
Looking up and over and down,
seat belt unfastened, the wind
not wind-fallen but blowing
through my capable hands, climbing
to the pinnacle of the Wheel
toward the golden aquarium
of the sun, and then down, down.

MIDNIGHT, THE CARRIAGE DEPARTS

When the sun dies down to moor in cinders behind
the Blue Mountains that follow me wherever I am,
blurring the frosted windowpane in the crimson
stockade of its ever-last light, I remember

how often toward morning you would enter
the reverie of my room, morning's grassy dew
brushstroking your footsteps as it were, and quench
and comfort me all the day long behind my door.

And I remember also, with the unbearable pain
that memory can so extravagantly, so darkly bring,
the last round ring of footsteps echoing into the ashes
of night, and the shattered slipper you left behind.

GLINN

For Love Of You

for love of you
two little hearts
open and close
their blossoms
in my wrists

Glimmer

as this flower opens
over night
while I'm asleep,
let me lightly touch
the rich, dark silence
I'd cut my wrists for.

The Viewing

Star through the window—
blue seashell five broken wings
on a bed of glass.

OPENING THE WINDOW

Opening the window
to let the air come in
and the darkness
on the dark wind...

not to lie alone
and isolate in the room
I opened the window
to let the night air in

but better I had remained
with you side by side alone
than to have let the darkness
join in with the wind

and gutter the light
and blanket the floor
the walls and the ceiling
the hours everything

THAT DARK PRINCE

Though that dark Prince has come
to harvest and bundle our body,

what matter, if the soul stays here
feasting on nasturtiums and poppies,

stays here gloried across this garden bed
which unlike the words we never shared

gave us the growing tenderness we had,
and despite our weather was the place we fed

And though that dark Prince would take away
my every joy and your every care

we will remain forever wholly ours
fluently mysterious and entirely fair

as proof the soul cannot be bartered or broken
into a threshing of elements to glean and bear

* *

And so Dark Prince of this our summer's end,
making hay with our body as your just dividend,

what matter to us, if the soul stays here
consonant in the frontier of its own delight,

carefully joining together in this poem's song
what no parting can tear apart, nor bid good-night

The Basement

There was a mummy that maybe was from a monastery or Mars,
          and Time had embalmed it with the image of each passer-by

There was a Cornell box with the music of the spheres
          playing a funeral dirge on a loom for Laertes and King Lear

A Rodin creation whose breasts were now discolored
          from the tobacco-stained fingers of the curator

There was a birdcage with Adam and Eve inside with a two-
          dimensional wormy apple suspended
                    above them, executed Calder fashion

And a chunk of a totem pole depicting some bygone spiritual-world
          organism as yet inhuman and undetermined

There were countless other things yet to be seen when I looked
          at my watch and noticed time was suspended

But I guessed it was about 3 hours since we had descended
          to the storage place where they kept their playthings

Then brushing the dust from my hair, I looked up searching
          for my lovely guide
                    and saw she had donned a bridal veil

And was now frozen still as a statue of herself in a wax museum
          from Hell

I wasn't sure how to resurface without her so I asked her
          to please lead the way up the channel to the door

She reluctantly agreed, and in a moment melted away into sunlight
          and thin air, leaving me alone in a multitude of earthenware

As I'm on display here now demonstrating for you
          what it's like to bear even the afterlife lightness
                    of a cobweb upon one's shoulder.

ALL SOULS' EVE
Vilnius

How do we know it is All Souls' Eve
when the wind's already thieved the calendar
through the steamy air of the kitchen,
out the window, and into the gutter.

My son waves why and goodbye, and the pages
of the years that were so happily engaged
a moment ago in the brisk furniture of air,
now barely flap their corners in despair.

Are they dead, he asks why, but really he says,
,and this prompts his sister to whirl, and flutter
her hands pretending that she is leaf and dove
let loose from a dark magic theatre above.

Brother, I can see the other side of life
where these yellow candles of my fingers
are dancing to sutartinės next to the stones,
and Christ's tears are turning to snow.

Sister, the calendar's in a pool of water,
does that mean that Time is dead
and why spirits will come to buzz by our bed
and feed us with mums and beebread.

Amazed by the strange talk of my children,
I bid them climb the chalk-white pony I'm riding,
and three Bellerophons on a lively errand
we fly to the graveyard to prance our bones,

to weep with Saint George for slaying the dragon,
and to kneel, three kids, before the chimera of Heaven.

Aurora Aurora

Fountain of the sun hovering in the West
before the hectic earth heaves and swallows it.
You're dreaming the snowy breasts, the soft footsteps
and languorous long arms of a Wyatt-like woman
come to break bread and drink new wine,
and her pregnant moon rising in the East,
plurabelle-emerald Springtime borne breath.

To awake from the fledging daydream is to pick up
broken, blue eggs from a storm-torn robin's nest
before dozing off again into a whisper of running water
from the Great Bear's dipper, and the svelte contours
and plumb-lined stars of evening, Venus before you
in her pinkly grim, voluptuous mourning gown.

Now, there's no vision of heaven or earth anymore,
of splendor in the grass, of glory in the flower,
or mortal intimation of immortal, celestial realms
other than the chirping, glad chorus of my children,
sweet Sonata's boneless, tumbling, yearling twins.
What will I do when they are through with this rheumy,
ancient, lopsided, soundless seashell of a poem-made man,
when they ship out of the Stygian marsh of my nursery room
to embrace the robin of the sun hatching in the blue mountains.

CRADLE SONG

for Myki and Kyva

No nanny no mommy
but daddy is here

Lulling you asleep
there's nothing to fear

Singing you swing low
and fish jumping too

Singing you Too-Ra-Loo-Ra
and pretty horses in a row

Singing you Jordan and Gilead
Valhalla and the Red Sea

Singing you mommy's heart
Singing you my artless soul

O' your eyes are like stars
your smiles pearly shells

Dream, dream on
your cradle my arms

Night's nestling balm
'til morning the sun

THE FOUNTAIN OF YOUTH

Only a stone's throw from the church of Saint Kotryna,
my happy-go-lucky children are throwing dozens of stones
into a broken-down fountain graced by the head of a lion.
I've told them nothing about desire and its vagrant wishes.
For them it's a game of getting wet and plips and splashes.
As for throwing coins for luck, they know nothing of this,
never suspecting anyone could be blessed in the heart of Vilnius.
Anyway, today I don't have any wisdom or coins to give them,
or obols or hunks of sea-washed amber or precious gems.
Besides, if these little Cyclopes had their way, they would plop rocks
or some looted, busted off piece of rococo or baroque.
Instead, I point out a few dandelions thrusting their sunny heads
through the dilapidated sidewalk, and like most kids
they already know what the dazzling florets will soon become,
resurrecting into the breathing of parachuting seeds of fuzzy cotton.
Like little gods, they are eager for some change or experiment,
so they don't at all mind my baptismal suggestion to "transplant"
the golden, severed heads into the fountain along with the stones
to see if they'll float like Christ or sink like an adulteress
        to the bottom—
an old man's gratuitous game. Fortunately, the young
        don't listen long,
and soon decide to take a bouquet of them back to their mom
to put in a tiny vase to regale the pallid parlor of their home,
where fittingly they will droop milkless and dead by morning.
But I'm getting too far ahead of myself. They're back
        with their stones
at the fountain with this would-be king of rock-throwers
        watching them
with admiration as grown-ups so often do, grown-ups addicted
to more Sisyphean and melancholy pastimes. Reverie
        can be seductive,
and soon I am far away from wherever I am, in some other land,
imagining myself picking myself up and throwing flesh and bones
over my own shoulder, turning into God's clay again
        or better yet, stone.

RECOGNITION

for Henry James

When the children were in their first few years,
I would go away each year to work for a month
to earn some bread, to keep us above board, the wolf away.
On returning, stepping in the door, they would peer
at me quizzically, as if through the mist at a stranger,
until I spoke their names or lifted them into my arms,
and then they seemed to remember a mask in a dream, and smile.
Though perhaps for myself or them, I could have been anyone,
and so it is now sometimes but with a different twist:
I'm at home, lost to myself, and someone comes to the door,
and obediently I answer, and as if in a slow motion film
welcome him home with a wry smile of recognition.
Then he gingerly steps across the threshold and I am gone.
Where to, who knows, but this happens again and again.

PLAYMATES

My daughter dreams of me at night,
and I daydream my childhood.
Perhaps we are playmates.

It's a seesaw of sorts.
I see her. She saw me.
She sees me. I saw her.

May the rhythm
go on up and down,
Earth and Heaven
in collaboration

In the dearest of dreams
dreaming us at play,
dawn to dusk,
dusk to dawn...

CHAINSONG

My son sings
his heartache
out in cheerless songs
he's chosen.

I know how
deep the heartache goes
in the chainsongs
of my poems.

"They fuck you up"
as Larkin said,
and put your heart
in pain,

parents that know
and don't know
what they do,
forgiven and unforgiven.

I wish for him
he escape his prison,
as I sawed to freedom
out of mine,

and never redoes
the night's light work
because there never
will be time.

No wise woman
will shipwreck
home
to rescue him,

no angel above or man
will be
his lion king
in heaven:

Son, as the key turns
in soul and mind,
the gate
swings open.

In Washington DC,
THINKING OF MY CHILDREN ACROSS THE OCEAN

for Matthew Olshan, the redbud man, and "after" Du Fu

Cherry blossoms crusted with snow.
Black ice shadows every step I go.
Two weeks since I've left you, seem years.
Such sadness burns up unwept tears.

Your mother writes me the fruit trees are dead,
left uncared for, unfenced, girded and fed
on by jackrabbits and bitter, winter wind.
The apple you took a bite out of, Kyva, fallen.

O' my daughter, is this what's come of any Eden.
And my son, will you soon transpire some new sin.
Never mind, before leaving, I planted a staghorn sumac
from the New World. Soon, I'll bring redbud pods back.

MY CHILDREN MARVEL AT THE WORD GREEN

and ask

is it a thing
does it look like gray

does it grow like the mold in the kitchen

on the walls of trees
that grow in the movies

they ask

if it is the dirt floor in the park
where the Labradors and the Rottweiler's poop

they ask why they are not allowed to go there
to touch it
the real green
to enter

and I look at them with pity in my heart
and I tell them

here I'll draw a copy of green for you: G R E E N
and you can touch it one letter at a time

and then they ask if green is a God
so still and dumb
and made out of paper and letters

and I tell them no green is not still and dumb
and yes green is a God
that endlessly echoes itself in a dirge

in the archives of a library
in a secret place far away
in another warp of space and time

and then they ask me what does dirge mean
and I tell them that dirge means green

READING AND WRITING CHRONICLE

Set this down:

Sunset on deck.
No stars yet.
Crows in silhouette
against antenna, chimneys, brick.
Last twittering flit
of swallows, a solitary bat
perching on the ledge
of its domicile
in the ghetto wall. Its
ancestors and their ancestors
perched there.
I turn the page.
Not a solitary Jew
on any balcony nearby.
It's not cold
but already a braid
of smoke
rises in a steady stream
from a neighbor's stove
into the sky.
I turn another page
Only last week
I saw a piece
of charred wood
in the courtyard below
and for a split-second
took it for a dead crow.
The sun sets.
I lay the book down
A first star, another.
The braid of smoke
about to disappear.
It's darker now.
For the moment
History's a closed book.
Tomorrow the sun
will come up
and similar shadows,
silhouettes, another poet
to rewrite it.
Another page
A different book